LEE KENDRICK

The Credit Score Game

It's Not Your Fault

...for everyone that's looking for a second chance in life!

~ Lee

Authenticity is everything! You have to wake up every day and look in the mirror, and you want to be proud of the person who's looking back at you. And you can only do that if you're being honest with yourself and being a person of high character. You have an opportunity every single day to write that story of your life.
~ Aaron Rodgers

Green Bay Packers, NFL Quarterback
& MVP of Super Bowl XLV

Contents

Preface

From an early age, I always observed the struggles of everyday life. And while I've certainly encountered my fair share of struggles through bad choices, indecision and bad timing... I've always felt a strong calling to helping people that life has beaten down.

Seeing the financial devastation that arises from small town manufacturing facility closures, medical events, addictions, divorce and numerous other financial burdens; I decided to learn everything I could about existing credit laws... and to extend a helping hand when possible.

Simply put... millions of people haven't received a solid financial education, proper advice or understand existing credit laws. So, this book has been written with you in mind.

After reading this book, applying much of what is written within and knowing what not to do in the future; you and your family should be better prepared by all the tomorrows.

Whatever you do... never give up! There is always hope.

Acknowledgement

I'd like to thank all the credit, banking, automotive and mortgage experts that have had an influence in my life, but it's impossible to name everyone. You know who you are… and I truly appreciate everything you've handed down to me and everyone else you've worked alongside in this fight to help everyone get better loan terms, save money and live a life with less worry and fear of loss.

The Secret Games They Play

What if I told you that numerous private and publicly traded corporations were profiting wildly... at your expense? How would you feel if I told you they were secretly collecting information about your shopping habits, medical bills, utilities, driving records, payment histories, etc. and then selling your data to the highest bidders? And what if they knew and didn't care that much of the information probably contains errors?

Would you be okay with having to spend untold hours of your time and hundreds (if not thousands) of your hard-earned dollars... to correct the errors, even though you didn't cause the errors or give them any bad information yourself?

Even worse, what if these HUGE corporations fought you tooth & nail... swearing that the erroneous data was verified as true & accurate?

Every day... millions of hard working people (like yourself) are denied credit, roped into paying higher interest rates or forced to challenge inaccurate, incomplete or unverifiable information that was collected or purchased by credit agencies.

And like it or not... these credit agencies & data behemoths are a part of your everyday life! And unless you've been living under a rock for the last 50+, I'm sure you'll recognize these company names... Equifax, Experian and TransUnion. And these buyers & sellers of your information… assign constantly changing scores (like it or not) that determine your fate!

Millions of people buy products of all types every day, such as: automobiles, houses, clothing, airline tickets, hotels, meals, etc. In exchange for your purchase, you receive something of value. If the product isn't to your satisfaction, you can usually exchange or return it for a refund.

But the system is broken because these huge corporations (the Big 3 credit reporting agencies) often receive bad information from creditors that sold or financed your purchases. And due to this weak link in the system… you can suffer from a bad credit rating, due to misinformation.

Equifax (aka CSC Credit Services), Experian and TransUnion (fka TRW) along with numerous lesser-known credit agencies (such as CoreLogic, Sagestream, LexisNexis, Certegy, DataX, etc. of which there at least 38) all collect, sell, share and report personal information about your past residences, nicknames, employment, shopping, gaming, utilities, loans, credit cards, mortgages, student loans, payment histories and much more. And much of this information can be erroneous, incomplete or unverifiable!

And these massive, for-profit corporations utilize TOP SECRET credit scoring formulas created by 3rd party companies, of which the 2 most widely used are from FICO (Fair Isaac & Company) or VantageScore. FICO is the 800-pound gorilla in the room, while VantageScore is quickly gaining steam behind the scenes.

Most people (even many credit industry experts) make an incorrect assumption or statement that the credit agencies assign your credit scores, but in reality they merely buy & sell your data that's contained

THE SECRET GAMES THEY PLAY

in your credit files. Then, every time a credit score is requested... in milliseconds, the credit agencies receive your calculated credit score from the licensed usage of the FICO, VantageScore or similar credit scoring formula.

Make sense? Fair?

It Depends Who You Ask

These massive credit agencies don't care, because your lower credit scores will result in more income due to more lenders having to review your credit requests (which they profit from every time a new credit request is submitted by a car dealership, mortgage lender, bank, finance company, credit card vendor, utility provider, mobile phone carrier, etc.)!

In case you didn't know... every business that checks your credit reports (when you request a loan or credit card) typically pays somewhere between $3-5 per credit bureau, per person.

So, if a car dealership submits your loan request (for you and your spouse) to 9 lenders (resulting in 10 credit report requests)... approximately $60-80 of revenue is generated by just ONE (1) credit agency. That's a whopping total of between $180-240 income (that happens in seconds) for all three (3) major credit corporations!

Picture this... if every US citizen over the age of 18 **only** applies for 1 piece of credit each year (which is average by the way), that's approximately 250,000,000 million people x 1 credit inquiry x 3 credit bureaus... equals 750,000,000 credit inquiries @ between $3-5 each, generates between $2,250,000,000 (yes, $2.25 BILLION) up to $3,750,000,000 PER YEAR!

That's staggering, flabbergasting and should open to your eyes to what's at stake... and explains 100% why these MASSIVE corporations don't want you to know about laws like the Fair Credit Reporting Act or to exercise your legal rights to challenge their data.

And why again??? They want more credit denials... so they can sell more credit reports! Especially since credit reports & scores are a complete mystery to most people.

Common Questions Abound...

Why does my credit score change every day? Why is Equifax showing different information than TransUnion? Why are the credit agencies reporting totally different credit scores? Why aren't my perfect auto loans from my local bank reporting on my credit reports? Why does CreditKarma.com show a different score than my Discover card? Why is the car dealership telling me credit score is lower? I took out a mortgage loan last week and they said my credit score was +80 points higher!

All these credit scoring formulas have created mass hysteria & consumer distrust within the credit arena... all because there's absolutely ZERO disclosure about how each of the credit scoring formulas (aka models) work.

You see, decades ago, these massive corporations ALSO decided to start pushing their own customized, tailor-made scoring formulas onto major lending institutions... selling them on the idea that their data could help these lenders be more competitive and profitable. Then lenders soon started making risk assessments based upon their very own secret, internal scoring formulas (unknown to consumers) based on data that's often corrupted, inaccurate, incomplete or unverifiable. And this also created additional revenue streams for these MASSIVE, soulless corporations!

Furthermore, all these various scoring formulas created a MAJOR problem on Wall Street in the late 90's thru the early-to-middle 2000's. But this is rarely mentioned by major media outlets, because the crash of 2007-2008 was blamed more on exotic loan programs that didn't require income documentation, full appraisals, etc. And while there were certainly some problems with those types of loans... the majority of those loans were only approved for people with better credit scores. Thus these exotic loans truly only accounted for a minority of originated loans.

The real problem was the fact that mortgage lenders regularly sell off chunks of loans to investors from Wall Street, major pension funds, utility companies, hedge funds, etc. These are known as mortgage backed securities aka "mortgage pools". However, Wall Street & other investors had absolutely no way of knowing the true risk of each mortgage pool... because each pool could've conceivably had hundreds (if not thousands) of different scoring formulas used PLUS credit scores also vary wildly from region-to-region in the US (7 different scoring regions). And it would've taken months for entire teams from investors to sift through each mortgage pool to determine its true risk.

Are you following me? A small percentage of loans were made without documentation... to people with great credit. But the majority of loans were made to credit types ranging from A+++ all the way down to D-, using full documentation of home values, income, etc.

The real culprit is thousands of different credit scoring formulas that clouded investors visions. And when mortgage pools began to under-perform... the house of cards collapse & dominoes began to fall.

And there's simply no incentive for them to change, because:

1) They're making money on the sale of your data,

2) and making money on EVERY credit report requested… often because of loan denials,

3) plus they're also profiting by selling secret scoring formulas to banks,

4) …and also charging people to monitor their own credit files!

This unethical abuse of power profits them at a mind-boggling $3-4 BILLION gross annual revenue at 22-28% net profit margins (equivalent to nearly $1 BILLION yearly net profits), which obviously isn't nearly sufficient enough (sic).

And don't even get me started about credit agency data breaches!

Credit Agencies Really Don't Suck

Up until the late 1980's to early 90's, it only mattered whether you paid your bills without being 30 days late. Credit scores simply weren't widely utilized. Loan requests were typically approved or denied after a manual credit review (which still happens today). But in the early-to-mid 90's almost every major lender published credit guidelines that incorporated credit scores... which determined the outcome of your loan request.

Credit agencies simply sold the banks on the idea that their data & attached credit scores could determine every bank's risk of loan default with greater precision than their human employees could... and with less expense. And true to their word... banks prospered!

But Why Don't Credit Agencies Suck?!

Picture this....

You live in the wrong section of town, or your employer has layoffs about once every year or two, everyone's been gossiping about your love life since your divorce or you had a medical emergency that caused some late payments.

Until the 1990's, your loan probably would've been denied OR you might've received terrible loan terms... all because of the human factor. Unless your family knew an officer of a local bank through church, the country club or their children's school.

Fast forward to today's day & age... your loan request usually isn't approved by a human anymore. And even if a human is manually reviewing your credit request, it's less likely that they even know anything about you personally... because you can obtain a loan from a lender that's 2,000 miles away (not in your hometown).

And because of the speed of today's technology, loan decisions are often computer generated in seconds... reducing interest rates and fees due to reduced expenses.

So, while there are certainly alot of problems with credit scoring formulas, data collection, data furnishing, etc... today's credit system is vastly superior to the days of old.

Now, I'm not saying there aren't any problems with the system... but it's definitely better than the alternative of possible discrimination, not having equal access to credit, etc.

I feel it's of utmost importance that we know who they purchase our data from, who they sell it to, how they compile it, what protective measures are in place to prevent fraud or hackers, why certain behaviors impact our scores so much, who can access our files, why social security numbers (or an exact match system) aren't required for access and what steps are they taking to reduce data compromises.

I have a monumental task & goal of educating and empowering millions of CreditUturn users with a complete knowledge of existing credit laws, how to get errors corrected, how data aggregation and compilers work, what's broken and find ways to fix it... for the betterment of ourselves, our neighbors as well as future generations.

When everyone's more educated, we all win!

The core basics to win in this high stakes game of credit, are as follows:
1) Pay your bills on time,
2) main low credit card balances in relation to each assigned credit limit,
3) reduce inquiries and only apply for credit when it's needed,
4) skip the 10% discount department card offers that are designed to induce spending,
5) establish and maintain a good mix of positive credit history,
6) prevent ID theft by monitoring your credits files,
7) and make sure all your personal info and account histories are accurate.

Approximately 8,000,000 credit disputes are filed each year! Huge number? Yes & no. Because it's relatively small in comparison to the 1,300,000,000 annual credit file requests that are submitted to the credit agencies, each year.

I think there should be more disputes, because numerous studies have been carried out by both federal and private watchdog agencies… that show anywhere between 20% to as high as 80% of all credit files have at least one (1) significant error that could impact whether your loan request is approved, declined or has less than desirable terms.

So, why only 8,000,000 disputes?

First of all, many consumers think that credit repair is a scam because they paid (an illegal) upfront fee to a scam artist… that never assisted them. And yes… they should rot in jail. Secondly, credit repair can be overwhelming if attempted on your own due to a lack of credit knowledge, persistence or laws. Thirdly, credit repair (even when legally performed) can be somewhat expensive (but far better than being stuck with higher interest rates, payments or being declined).

Well... I've got a news flash!

Credit repair isn't a scam, it's not illegal, the Fair Credit Reporting Act of 1971 give you the right to challenge inaccurate, incomplete and unverifiable credit data. So, you either need to educate yourself, be persistent and know your rights.

Or download the CreditUturn app & get started on your journey to better credit, today!

The History of Credit Reporting

If we lived in a world where banks didn't offer credit to people or businesses… we probably wouldn't enjoy all the glorious technology, automobiles, computers, skyscrapers, malls, etc. that we all enjoy the use of every day.

Would there be some benefit? Possibly.

But overall growth is often dependent upon the ability of people and corporations to obtain funding that's needed to buy, build, advertise and prosper.

In a cash only environment, even if you make alot of money on a regular basis… there isn't any proof of your desire or ability to repay a new loan. In fact, some of the wealthiest people on this planet often have bad credit ratings… because they won't pay someone until they're sued. And even then, they'll often bankrupt small businesses that can't afford to get the legal help they need to recover damages from the multi-millionaire!

And this is exactly why a credit reporting system exists!

Without it, a cash only payer hasn't demonstrated a willingness or desire to repay… so this is why they're considered a bad credit risk. Yet, logically, it doesn't make sense either. Why isn't someone rewarded for living within their means, paying for everything in cash, and even investing their savings into stocks as well as other business opportunities?

These concerns eventually led to the creation of credit agencies and the current rules they operate within. Who makes the rules? The credit agencies & their lobbyists… in large part.

In the early days, credit agencies were local… not national or international. Grocery stores, retailers and banks established small credit bureaus that operated under a shroud of secrecy. Consumer details were recorded onto manual paper ledgers, often in pencil. If a stranger applied for store credit, an employee would often run down the street or ride across town to ask whether someone was a good credit risk… and it was all very subjective, often prejudiced and time consuming. Even worse, there wasn't any specific criteria or rating system to determine someone's true credit worthiness.

And, unlike today's day & age… you had ZERO rights to view your credit files or to dispute any erroneous information that you may have heard of.

Way back then, they even collected your marital status, sexual persuasion, religion, testimonials, employment history, income history, race, age, criminal history, etc. Discrimination was rampant!

The Welcome Wagon's Role in the Credit Industry

And even all the way up until the 1980's, the local chapter of the Welcome Wagon would make house calls to welcome new neighbors into communities. On the surface, visits from 2-3 women employed by the local Welcome Wagon chapter seemed very charitable. However, they were really only reporting everything about your family, photographs, furnishings, etc. directly back to the local credit bureau. Think local gossiping tattlers!

Associated Credit Bureaus (ACB)

In 1906, the Associated Credit Bureaus (ACB) was established to improve the sharing of information from local credit bureaus. And it's membership grew quickly, which basically laid the foundation for the formation of the major credit agencies we know today.

The Fair Credit Reporting Act of 1971

By the time the 1950's and 1960's rolled around… credit cards had gained popularity, but many banks suffered from poor credit decisions, due to poorly reported data. Plus, the federal government was hearing loud complaints of housing loan discrimination. So, in 1971 the federal government took action and created the Fair Credit Reporting Act of 1971, also known as the FCRA.

This led to an initial reform of the credit agencies data collection, storage and reporting practices. And while they became more reliable throughout the decades, the weak link has always been the platforms that the data is sent on or received by… leading to inaccuracies, incomplete reporting, and unverifiable or obsolete account information.

FICO

The Fair, Isaac and Company (FICO) completely revolutionized the credit reporting industry in the 1980's… via its automated, numerical risk assessment formulas. Depending upon scoring formulas in place today, FICO scores range anywhere between 300 (on the low side) up to 850 (for mortgages) and 900 (for auto loans).

The average FICO scores vary somewhat throughout 7 different regions of the United States, typically between the range of 680-695. And approximately 50% of all FICO scores are between the 650-799 score range.

The advent of the FICO scoring system helped credit agencies demonstrate that they wanted to reduce discriminatory lending practices and it helped them eliminate further government oversight.

And while the FICO credit scoring system has certainly reduced discrimination, opened up more access to credit options, and sped up the underwriting process… it also fails millions of borrowers each year.

Since banks don't rely on manual underwriting much anymore, a simple $42 water bill collection might cause your credit scores to drop 60, 80 or 100+ points. This could cause you to pay thousands in additional interest charges or to be denied credit completely!

Furthermore, FICO results can often provide really wacky scores of 700+ for 18 year old borrowers with a small credit card that barely has any reported history. Whereas, someone with 30+years of positive credit history can have a medical bill drop their credit scores 100+ points or more… that they might not have even known about!

Plus some market indicators point to a strong possibility that faulty FICO risk assessments played a significant role in the mortgage crisis of 2007 and 2008.

And remember… there isn't much incentive for the credit agencies to change it either. Credit denials just help the Big 3 credit agencies to earn their BILLIONS in annual revenue!

FICO Score Metrics

- 35% Payment History
- 30% Balance-to-Limit Ratios
- 15% Length of Credit History
- 10% Recent Inquiries
- 10% Mix of Credit Types

VantageScore

In recent years, the Big 3 credit agencies decided that they were going to put there heads together to create their own scoring model known as the VantageScore… as a direct competitor to FICO. Their reasoning was two-fold, 1) eliminate paying fees to FICO every time a credit score was issued due to a credit request and 2) they felt that they could develop a more accurate prediction of bankruptcy risks.

It assessed credit file information in much the same way as FICO, but it also assigns a letter as well as numerical grade. VantageScore 3.0 will return score ranges from 300-850… while the earliest scoring model range was 501-990. The current average VantageScore is reported as being 673, as of November 2018.

VantageScore 3.0 Metrics
- 32% Payment History
- 23% Balance-to-Limit Ratios
- 13% Credit History
- 10% Recent Inquiries
- 15% Total Open Balances
- 7% Total Available Credit

The VantageScore is becoming more and more utilized by lenders behind the scenes (in secret). But the primary score that most car dealerships, mortgage brokers and finance companies see are still FICO driven results.

After every credit request, lenders must provide you with a Risk Based Pricing Disclosure that shows you at least one of your current credit scores, where you rank accordingly among all consumers, which credit agency has reported that score and also provides you with credit agency contact info and also explains a brief summary of your rights.

Intellectual Property Violations and Lawsuits

In the wake of all this drama, FICO has filed massive lawsuits alleging collusion and intellectual property violations against all 3 major credit agencies… stating that the credit bureaus abused their access to FICO's proprietary scoring formulas. Grab your popcorn, because it's going to get crazy!

Equifax

Equifax was founded in 1899, operates in 14 countries and generated gross revenues in excess of $3.8 Billion dollars ($3,800,000,000) in 2017… which is a massive increase from only (sic) $1.9 Billion in 2011.

Equifax is headquartered in Atlanta (GA) and manages a whopping 400,000,000+ million individual consumer files… more than the US population!

In 2017, Equifax was rocked by alleged insider trading after numerous executives sold stock after they were informed that hackers had gained access to and stolen information from nearly 200,000,000 credit files… and it happened again in 2018 too. Sheesh!

And being no stranger to scandals… Equifax was discovered to have operated a cash incentive program in the 1960's and 70's that rewarded employees who discovered negative information about consumers. This predatory pattern of discrimination & "holier than thou" attitude from Equifax isn't anything new... and really doesn't surprise me!

Experian

Experian employs more than 15,000 people in 37 countries worldwide. In 2017, Experian produced $4.3 Billion in gross revenue, and manages more than 1,000,000,000 individual and business records... which include more than 235,000,000 U.S. consumers and 25,000,000 U.S. businesses.

And although it has the ability to affect U.S. citizens' loan decisions... their headquarters are in Dublin, Ireland and its main offices are located in Nottingham, England.

Experian was created by a combination of buyouts and consolidations, getting most of their original data from the purchase of TRW Information Systems... which was one of the United States of America's oldest credit agencies. Since then, Experian has continued its aggressive shopping spree... by purchasing and expanding into the email marketing, digital data mining, debt consolidation, collection and surveillance industries too! Experian obviously has its eye on providing much more than just credit reports.

TransUnion

TransUnion is a privately held company, so they don't have to publicly declare its annual revenue or other private company information. We do know it got started in the credit industry when it bought out the Cook County Credit Bureau (of Chicago, Illinois)... which was one of the original and largest Welcome Wagon locations in the United

States.

TransUnion's headquarters are still located in Chicago, Illinois... although much of its dispute processing is administered from Crum Lynne, PA (just outside of Philadelphia). TransUnion also outsources most of its credit disputes through companies like ACS/Xerox and from a location in the Philippines.

Legal Drama

All 3 of the credit agencies are no strangers to legal defeats. After just a little bit of search engine research, you'll quickly discover numerous instances of private individuals receiving jury awards in excess of $3,000,000 for a credit agency's role in disregarding an individual's right to only having 100% accurate, complete and verifiable information contained in their credit files.

As noted previously, Equifax has had recent data breaches that went undisclosed for weeks or months. And in 2000, the Federal Trade Commission (FTC) fined all 3 major credit agencies for willfully violating the Fair Credit Reporting Act. The FTC found that Equifax, Experian and TransUnion were intentionally blocking and/or delaying phone calls, faxes and other types of correspondence from consumers... who were simply trying to obtain their rightfully owned credit information.

But, the fine was a complete joke!

Imagine this: 3 major corporations that collectively earn in excess of $10 Billion dollars annually... being fined a total whopping amount of only $2,500,000 dollars!! What??? That's absolutely ridiculous!

That's kind of like you earning $100,000 per year & only being fined $25 after you critically injured someone will intentionally driving straight at them.

Since then… nothing much has changed, except easier access to credit files. They simply don't have any financial fear. And until they do… they'll simply continue to not care about the actual integrity of the data that they're scoring and reselling every minute, every day.

Slaying the Giants

Until recently, everyone always assumed or was led to believe that credit disputes cost the credit agencies millions of dollars, annually. But... it's not true! Based on congressional hearings, sworn testimony and insider information; *the truth is that credit agencies actually PROFIT from the dispute process.*

Remember when I demonstrated how credit agencies profit the most from customers with poor credit histories, because more credit requests are made every time a consumer with poor credit is denied for a loan? And considering that the very same credit agencies are also in charge of correcting your disputed credit files... it's the classic story of hiring the fox to guard the hen house. You simply don't do it!

Zero Incentive to Make Accurate

And since negative data is more valuable than the accurate data... the credit agencies have ZERO incentive to update credit files to make them 100% accurate, complete and verifiable. The small fines simply don't motivate them to correct their shady ways of doing business. And banks need their data & formulas too much for Congress to truly do anything about it.

Rights Contained in the (FCRA) Fair Credit Reporting Act

You have the right to dispute inaccurate, incomplete or unverifiable information. And the credit agency must investigate all disputed information (unless its frivolous), using a clearly defined process that's outlined within the FCRA. Once it's been determined that you're dispute is valid, the information must be permanently removed from your credit files within thirty (30) days. And negative information that's outdated must also be deleted, regardless of whether it was disputed by a consumer or not.

The Math

Outsourcing by the credit agencies has slashed expenses so far... that it's actually become a source of revenue! Equifax' cost per dispute was $4.67, until 2004. After Equifax began utilizing an outsourcing vendor (ACS) in Montego Bay, Jamaica... ACS investigations only cost Equifax $1.08 each. But that wasn't enough... because a different outsourcing vendor (DDC) a Filipino agency has reduced costs to only $0.57 per dispute... dispute the volume of dispute requests from credit repair companies!

It's been estimated that the typical U.S. consumer has five (5) errors in their credit file.

So assuming you mailed one (1) dispute letter for all five (5) errors. The credit agency will then forward it to the overseas-based outsourcing vendor and pays them $0.49 to investigate all 5 errors.

Now this gets really interesting, because the credit agencies actually CHARGE a fee to the data furnishers (example, MBNA) for providing inaccurate data. Each item disputed will result in a $0.25 fee, per bureau. So, the credit agency charges $1.25 to the creditors that have reported items incorrectly... which results in a $0.76 profit on a $0.49 investment.

That's a return of 155% on your investment! Wouldn't you love to get $155 back for every time that you gave someone $100... and within less than 30 days?!

And that my fine friends... is how the rich get richer & the poor get poorer!

You Have Rights!

Utilize your Fair Credit Reporting Act rights outlined above (seemingly simple enough) to force the credit agencies to investigate your claims... and sleep well knowing that they're also profiting from your disputes, your credit requests and the sale of your personal data.

CreditUturn Dispute Automation

And if you haven't already done it... download the CreditUturn mobile app, to simplify, control and automate your credit repair and rebuilding journey!

It's easy to manage, fun and empowering too!

Bankruptcy Risk Indicator What?

News flash! The term credit score is much sexier than "Bankruptcy Risk Indicator Score"! No doubt... Sherlock!

When FICO first provided its top-secret credit scoring formula as a solution to the deep doo-doo that the credit agencies were in, due to the credit agencies' recent discriminatory practices... they weren't all that impressed _with the name_. A bankruptcy risk indicator score simply wasn't going to be sexy enough to get banks to part with their money.

So, after just a little brainstorming... credit scores were born & pushed forth into the world!

But in reality, now that you're learning this tidbit of trivia... doesn't it all make more sense? When you apply for a loan, the main thing the banks want to know isn't whether you'll be late (at least not primarily)... because they're more concerned about your likelihood of filing for Chapter 7 bankruptcy protection, causing them all kinds of additional legal fees, lost interest earnings, lost principle (the money you borrowed) and the headaches associated with explaining to the bank's investors (shareholders) why its quarterly and annual earnings report is looking so bad.

So, whenever you're considering applying for a loan... ask yourself if you appear likely to file bankruptcy or not. And then you'll have a better understanding of why your "Credit score" might be lower or higher than expected.

And for the record, low credit scores aren't good… even if it's increased from a 388 to a 520. Remember the basics and you'll be on a path to 700+ or 800+ scores, as follows:

FICO Score Metrics
- 35% Payment History
- 30% Balance-to-Limit Ratios
- 15% Length of Credit History
- 10% Recent Inquiries
- 10% Mix of Credit Types

Credit Report Analysis

And now you have a better understanding of what is trying to be accomplished by FICO or VantageScore credit formulas... which is to assign a 3-digit credit score, as an indicator for a potential creditor to determine the likelihood that you'll file a bankruptcy.

And because of this, the rest of your credit analysis becomes much easier to understand. So, let's look at the various components of your credit report. A typical credit report is broken down into the following sections, as follows:

- Personal Info - names, addresses, aliases, birthdates & Social Security numbers
- Credit Score - a 3-digit numerical bankruptcy risk indicator
- Fraud Alert - declaring an ID theft risk & your request for phone confirmation
- Public Records - bankruptcies, tax liens and judgments
- Collections - primarily medical, utility and municipal debts
- Consumer Statement - an up to 100 word reply, to disputes that agencies denied
- Open Accounts - some American Express cards & child support payments
- Revolving Accounts - credit cards & home equity credit lines (not equity loans)
- Installment Debt - auto, home, personal and student loans
- Inquiries - shows the date & which creditors processed your credit request

Personal Info

Your personal info section is of incredible importance!

First of all, the more similar your personal information is across all three (3) major credit agencies... the higher your credit scores will be. Why? Because the 3 major agencies know there's less likelihood of corrupted data and/or identity theft... if there aren't different addresses, names, aliases, birthdates, and social security numbers.

Secondly, when you're able to get inaccurate, incomplete or unverifiable names, aliases, addresses, birthdates and social security numbers deleted from your credit files... it makes it more difficult for credit agencies and/or creditors to match you to other reported account information that are utilizing inaccurate, incomplete or unverifiable personal identifiers that you have successfully disputed. Therefore, disputed account information will often be removed easier... due to their inability to match the accounts to any existing personal identifying information that is still being reported by the credit agencies.

Credit Score (aka Bankruptcy Risk Indicator Score)

This is the section of your credit report that will display your 3-digit numerically assigned credit score, also known as your Bankruptcy Risk Indicator Score.

Please, remember that this score is NOT assigned to you by the credit agency itself... as they pay FICO a licensing fee every time a new credit score is generated. And, your score can change every time any data or information in your credit report changes. So, your score is always fluid... not assigned or static.

Fraud Alert

The credit agencies will add a FRAUD ALERT (usually in ALL CAPS lettering) that's prominently displayed in your credit report... stating that you've been the victim of fraud or identity theft & requesting your phone confirmation before approving any credit requests.

Public Records

The Public Records section of your credit report will typically display the name and location of the public courthouse or records facility (along with the book & page number) that you can find the recorded bankruptcy, tax lien or civil judgment information.

Recently, many credit agencies have stopped reporting tax lien and civil judgment information in your credit reports. However, lenders can still discover tax liens and civil judgments by purchasing special types of credit reports that the credit agencies charge extra fees to access... or also through a public records search by a title research clerk.

Remember this if you're planning to purchase or sell land or a house... as the discovery of an outstanding tax lien and/or civil judgment may prevent the transaction unless you have sufficient funds to pay it in full or the plaintiff is willing to waive their right to a first lien purchase on the new property being purchased (which is rare).

Collections

This section is probably the most self-explanatory section because it only displays information about collection accounts from places like hospitals, utility companies, mobile carriers and municipal offices.

However, it seems like most consumers have little to zero remembrance of most collection accounts... and sometimes with good reason.

Consumer Statement

A consumer can submit up to a 100-word "consumer statement" to be displayed close to the account that was verified as accurate by the credit agency.

As an example, a general consumer statement such as: "I was unable to receive billing statements while deployed overseas while serving in the US Air Force from Aug 2016 thru February 2018." can also be added to your credit reports in a section that's usually displayed closer to your personal information.

Open Accounts

This section displays your open accounts that require payment in full, each month. These types of accounts are typically only certain types of American Express card or child support payments (as your $600 monthly child support bill is considered due in full each month).

Revolving Accounts

The revolving credit section typically displays only credit card debt & home equity lines of credit (not to be confused with a home equity loan that requires the same payment amount every month). Balances owed for credit cards and home equity lines of credit can vary every month, as the balances can increase as well as decrease... depending upon how much you charge and pay off each month.

The total number of revolving accounts, the credit limits for each (as well as total amount of available credit), the balances of each and your overall utilization (balance-to-limit percentages)... are of utmost importance to your credit scores!

It's recommended that you have at least 2-3 open credit cards (not closed), with minimum credit limits of at least $2,500 on each credit card, and keep your open balances paid below 30% of your credit limits (preferably between 1% to 10% of your limits, for best results). And you should NEVER be in the habit of charging the full limit & then paying it off every month... because your credit report scores might be generated during a period when your credit cards appear to be maxed out. If this happens... you look like a total bankruptcy risk!

Installment Accounts

This section displays your auto, home, personal and student loan history. The creditor name, account number, date opened, last date reported, date of last activity, loan term, the monthly payment amount, current account balance, any amount past due, number of months rated (or reviewed) as well as the last 2 years of payment history (indicating whether you were 30, 60, 90, 120, 150, included in bankruptcy, repossessed or the account was charged off for tax purposes due to default) will be shown for each account.

The same type of information is also reported for each of your revolving accounts, within the revolving account section.

Inquiries

Every time you apply for credit a potential lender checks your credit, reviews your residence history (or lack thereof), your income (ability to repay the loan), your job stability (time on the job), sources of income (are you likely to continue earning the income for the whole loan term), the loan collateral (is the value of the car similar to or less than the requested loan amount) and whether you are paying any cash toward the purchase of the car (demonstrating a strong commitment toward repayment of the debt)

And when credit checks are performed, each potential creditor's is displayed in the bottom section of your credit report & is also date stamped. Additionally, credit requests are often initiated by car dealerships with numerous potential lenders… even moreso if you've had significant credit challenges. You can request a limit to the number of credit requests they make and/or to exact lenders.

Just be cautious if you do this, because you might restrict them from submitting to a lender that may have given you more favorable terms. I see numerous instances of this every month, where consumers with 800+ credit scores will demand the use of a particular bank… yet could've saved 1-2% percentage points off their interest rate if they would've allowed the car dealership to help them select better terms.

And another credit myth is that the car dealership "ruined my credit score" because they "shotgunned" my credit application to 20+ banks.

First of all, you already had credit problems of some type (bad credit scores, owed more than your trade was worth, had borrowers that lived at 2 different addresses, etc, etc).

Secondly, there's a federal law that makes the credit agencies only score all those one-time event inquiries as ONE (1) INQUIRY as long as they occurred within a 14-day window.

Lastly, credit inquiries only affect 10% of your credit score. Plus they only stay on your credit report for two (2) years, and once they've aged more than one (1) year they even carry lesser weight.

Are You Creditworthy?

Even if you have a 720-850 credit score... you can still be denied credit! Seriously? Why?!!
- Do you have enough monthly income?
- Will your income continue for the entire loan term? Child support & settlements.
- Do you carry too much debt in proportion to your regular income?
- Are you trying to borrow $30,000 for a $20,000 car?
- Do you already have a bunch of open auto or recreational loans?
- Are you starting to max out credit cards?
- Do you have multiple mortgage loans? It's a red flag to some lenders.
- Have you had a bunch of recent credit inquiries?
- Do you have a Fraud Alert warning on your credit report?
- Do you have a Consumer Statement in your credit files?
- Did you co-sign for someone that filed for bankruptcy protection?

These are just some of the reasons why even borrowers with great credit scores can be declined credit, when needed. Being more aware of this should help you better prepare your overall financial picture, so you'll be considered more creditworthy when you apply.

Creditworthiness is as much about your ability to repay a debt, your residence and job stability as well as your equity or commitment that you're bringing to the table.

Here's an easy analogy to remember… to help you better prepare!

C-A-S-E

Always remember the acronym "C-A-S-E"… which stands for:
- Credit - What is your overall credit report picture & credit score?
- Ability - Your ability to repay debt, which is your available disposable income
- Stability - Do you move alot or change jobs often?
- Equity - Are you borrowing less than or close to the value of the car or home?

So let's simplify it even further. Picture a table with 4 legs, and each table is labeled "C" for Credit, "A" for Ability, "S" for Stability, and "E" for Equity.

Now, when you remove 1 of the 4 table legs… does the table still stand? Sure it does.

1) So when you remove ANY single 1 of these items, you'll still more than likely (not as easily as when all 4 legs are attached) be able to find a lender for your loan.

2) What happens when you remove ANY 2 of these table legs? The table sure wobbles alot more, and you'll have about a 50% chance of getting a loan approval. But your loan terms certainly won't be the best.

3) What happens when you remove 3 of these table legs? The table might stand momentarily if it was balanced "just right", but the tiniest wobble… and it collapses right before your eyes! The same holds true with your loan request, when you remove ANY 3 of the same 4 table legs. So, yes there's probably only a 1%-10% chance (not

25% as you might be thinking) that your loan would be approved. In this situation… it's usually because CASH IS KING. Some "hard money" lenders, finance companies, loan sharks, buy-here pay-here lots, etc. might be willing to approve your risky loan request if they have absolutely nothing to lose… but nowadays most lenders still think it's not worth the probable nightmare that follows with collection phone calls, letters, legal maneuvers, etc.

4) And when all 4 table legs are missing… everybody declines your loan requests.

The CreditUturn mobile app can't fix your income, stability or down payments. But the wisdom, advice and support (plus a little real talk or tough love) you'll receive from the CreditUturn Facebook private members community is priceless!

Lastly, verifiable documentation of your income and/or residence is often needed nowadays. And self-employed borrowers have lending options that often allow 3-6 months of your most recent bank statements to verify your gross monthly deposits. Just be aware that the lender will also look to see if you've had any overdraft or insufficient fund charges.

Who Can View My Credit Reports?

A federal law that's been in existence since 1971, known as the Fair Credit Reporting Act (FCRA), strictly limits who can access your credit report and under what circumstances.

The FCRA lists these specific, permissible reasons for others to view your credit report:
- in accordance with your written instructions (credit application);
- in response to a court order or federal grand jury subpoena;
- to manage the risk of current or potential credit or insurance accounts that were initiated by you (to determine possible credit limit adjustments);
- for employment purposes, from your signed employment application;
- for the purposes of a potential investor assessing your current debt obligations;
- in connection with your application for a license or other benefit granted by the government, when consideration of financial responsibility is required by law;
- in connection with a business transaction initiated by an individual;
- in connection with a child support determination, under certain circumstances;
- when "firm offer" of credit or insurance is extended, also known as a "soft pull".

Your permission is not required in every instance.

As an example, your credit history may be accessed without your approval in order to make a preapproved credit offer. But a notice that your credit history will be accessed, is typically provided with credit applications... often stating that by signing credit application you will give the lender permission to view your credit reports.

You can greatly reduce access to your credit history by businesses that send preapproved credit offers by calling 1-888-567-8688 (1-888-5OPTOUT). Doing this will prevent you from receiving mailed preapprovals... but only for 5 years.

To permanently stop receiving junk, preapproved credit offers... you'll need to go to https://optoutprescreen.com, complete the online request form, print it out and then mail it in. Or in the near future, you can simply choose the 'Stop Junk Mail' feature in the CreditUturn mobile app, and CreditUturn will submit it for you!

And we highly recommend opting out of the Direct Marketing Association's list too! There are three (3) ways you can opt-out of the Direct Marketing Association's lists, as follow:

1. You can complete and submit their online form for $2 at www.DMAChoice.org, which will only block junk mail for 10 years. However, you can choose which types of mail you do or don't want to receive.
2. You can also register through its DMA eMail Preference Service... to reduce your unsolicited commercial email.
3. Or you can **permanently** opt-out by filling out the DMAChoice Mail In Form with all the required information, print it, attach a $3 check or money order (made payable to 'DMA') and mail it to: **DMAChoice, PO Box 900, Cos Cob, CT 06807.**

Give careful thought to opting out, though. When you opt out of receiving preapproved credit offers you're essentially removing yourself from the credit marketplace. That can significantly reduce your access to credit services you may want or need in the future, that you might like to have but weren't aware of.

However, I firmly believe that it's better to only apply for credit when it's needed… instead of always being tempted to apply for new offers that magically appear in your mailbox. Preapproved credit offers tend to have too much fine print, higher rates or subprime terms.

Think of it this way. With better credit, you're more likely to be able to get what you want… when you want it!

How Did That Get There?

When you apply for credit, lending institutions have permission to submit an electronic request for your credit files…. **which crazily does not require your Social Security number!** The credit agencies will return your credit report results to the lender, even though they could've entered an incorrect Social Security number.

As an example: when a Social Security number (such as 123-45-6789) is entered incorrectly, the lender will see an alert that there is a Social Security mismatch.

But an identity theft risk of GIGANTIC proportions exists because of this! And the credit agencies' refusal to require either 8 or 9 matching digits, leaves the door wide open for Identity Theft… and more credit agency profits!

Credit Monitoring Income

All 3 major credit agencies offer credit monitoring services… that lull the general public into thinking that they're helpless versus identity thieves, yet promise to notify them when someone applies for credit in their name. And this is exactly how the credit monopolies have figured out how to make money… from people with great credit too!

Most people with bad credit, simply won't spend money on credit monitoring unless it's an absolute necessity… because they don't fear someone stealing their bad credit rating.

Yet, people with great credit will pay almost anything to protect their credit!

The credit agencies collectively earn more than $1 Billion annually from the sale of credit monitoring services, both directly and indirectly to consumers. The credit agencies also own other websites (such as Experian's FreeCreditReport.com) that consumers might not be aware of. And most of these sites don't really offer free credit reports… just short trial periods that require credit cards which convert into monthly paid subscriptions.

And until the advent of paid credit monitoring services, the "great credit" market segment just wasn't profitable. People with excellent credit ratings didn't apply for credit as often, and typically didn't have their loan requests submitted to as many lenders… which had resulted is less revenue for the credit agencies.

In its annual report to shareholders, on May 23, 2017… Experian proclaimed:

> *"Consumer Direct (online credit reports, scores and monitoring services) delivered excellent growth throughout the period, with strong demand from consumers for credit monitoring services, which led to higher membership rates."*

However… the FCRA and/or FACTA (the Fair and Accurate Credit Transactions Act) states that consumers are able to obtain one free credit report within sixty (60) after a consumer has been denied credit, insurance or employment; if the consumer is unemployed and is seeking employment; or if the consumer suspects fraud or identity theft.

Therefore, when FreeCreditReport.com (owned by Experian) is charging consumers an annual or monthly subscription fee for services that consumers can otherwise receive for free (in the circumstances outlined in the previous paragraph)… it is essentially useless and redundant for consumers.

Secondly, consumers are also entitled to completely freeze their credit reports (and receive a Identity Theft Prevention PIN #) for a low one-time of only $5. This is the ultimate in identity theft prevention… yet it's rarely ever mentioned on any advertisements, which you'd think the Federal Trade Commission , the Attorney General, the Bureau of Consumer Financial Protection or state Attorney Generals would squash.

Isn't Credit Report Accuracy an FCRA Right?

On Equifax's website homepage, Equifax sells its credit monitoring services by stating "Make sure your reports are accurate & free of fraud."

Imagine a hospital that advertised a paid service which guaranteed patient confidentiality. Aren't hospitals required by a federal law (HIPPA) to safeguard patients' medical records anyway? It's complete and utter nonsense… and only exists to boost their bottom line!

But credit reporting agencies aren't the only culprits, because one of the largest tax preparation services in the U.S. (H&R Block) offers an upgrade to a paid insurance product that reimburses you if the tax preparer makes an error on your filed income tax return.

Identity Theft Data

In 2011, the FTC reported nearly 280,000 identity theft complaints in the United States... yet almost 50% of these complaints were actually determined to be credit report inaccuracies... which is nearly enough to make the credit agencies the #1 FTC complaint.

Why are there so many instances of inaccurate data?

A recent study by the National Credit Reporting Association, in conjunction with the Consumer Federation of America, found that slightly more than 10% of 1,545 mortgage applicants' credit reports... contained at least 1 and up to 3 additional consumers' information.

In simpler language... a complete stranger's (or as many as 3 other people's) BAD CREDIT were mixed into 155 (out of 1545) mortgage applicants' credit reports. **What??! How?!!**

Common Reasons for Mixed Credit Files

Mixed credit files can happen because of numerous things, such as:
1. family name suffixes are mixed between Jr., Sr., II, III, IV, V, etc.
2. similar names, but different Social Security numbers
3. files with similar Social Security numbers, but different names
4. applicant's report showing accounts from co-applicant's Social Security number
5. co-applicant's report showing accounts from applicant's Social Security number
6. transposed first and middle name variations
7. transposed first and last names
8. transposed middle and last name variations
9. hyphenated last names
10. files that tracked unknown or duplicate accounts also in applicant's nickname
11. spelling errors in names
12. transposed digits in Social Security numbers

13. similar addresses, but different Social Security numbers

It's 2018 and self-driving cars are on our roadways. Which is why it's so hard to believe that the credit agencies still haven't fixed these problems. Or is it?? Hmmmm...

Remember.. it's in their best interest to have bad information being reported. Right?! Because credit agencies profit wildly... when more credit requests have to be made, due to borrowers' credit denials. Sad, but true!

The Equifax Deposition Confirmation... For the Win!

And just so you don't think I'm some sort of wild conspiracy theorist... here's a summary of a deposition (in 2005) of Equifax's Vice President of Technology.

Question: And what is required to match a tradeline to an existing credit file?

Answer: We use the L90 search logic, which has thirteen (13) matching elements, and based on those thirteen matching elements, we have an internal algorithm that makes the determination whether the ID matches sufficiently to apply the trade.

Question: If a first and last name and the full Social Security number on the tradeline match an existing file, would Equifax report that tradeline to the existing file?

Answer: Yes, given there was not other information that was in conflict that prevented that, that kind of took away from the positive match of a name and a Social then, yes, I believe it would. I would like to see the specific example, though.

Question: What if the current address is on the existing file and the new tradeline did not match?

Answer: If the Social Security number matches, that's normally enough information to allow it to update, even if the address does not match.

Wait... What???? Wow!! A full match of your data isn't necessary for creditor information to appear in your credit report. That's ridiculous... and now you know how that got there!

Online, Mail or Fax?

It seems like the newest thing that credit agencies and various credit monitoring websites like CreditKarma.com are offering nowadays are online disputes. But they've simply figured out another way to make it easier on themselves... and to defraud the public! And they even have the gumption to pretend it's a consumer friendly mechanism... which unfortunately federal regulators have also bought hook, line and sinker.

Their online dispute systems force the consumer to log onto their websites, enter or select the accounts they wish to dispute, choose the reason for each of their disputes (from a list), agree to their website Terms & Conditions of use (which state that by using the online dispute portal that the consumer forfeits their rights to sue the credit agency) and then click to submit their disputes.

Once that process is completed, the consumer's disputes are immediately converted into a 3-digit code (not to be confused with your credit score), and then that code is forwarded to the credit agency's investigation department. Decisions to correct, remove or verify the disputed accounts can be made within minutes to days... and a human never reads any attached, supporting documents!

This process appears to benefit consumers... until you realize that the convenience of selecting dispute items and not having to write a letter actually strips some valuable rights from the consumer, that are afforded to consumers within the Fair Credit Reporting Act… as outlined below.

30-Day Time Limit

Using the credit agencies' online dispute portals, to digitally file a credit complaint, makes it very easy for credit bureaus to respond to consumer disputes without conducting a truly full investigation… in minutes to days.

However, if a consumer mails or faxes a written dispute letter with supporting documentation the credit agencies' online dispute system is bypassed… forcing credit bureaus to forward the dispute AND ALL SUPPORTING DOCUMENTATION to the creditor.

And when credit agencies are unable to resolve consumer disputes within 30 days… the disputed information must be permanently deleted from your credit files.

Paper Trail

You have a right to choose how you want to dispute any of your credit report information. And by choosing to mail or fax your disputes… you can document a paper trail easier, if needed to file a lawsuit against creditors and/or credit agencies.

More Dispute Choices

The coding system that is utilized by the credit agencies' online dispute portals is very limited to the choices that they display. And there isn't really enough character space for you to properly explain and/or provide evidence why a tradeline should be fixed or deleted. How can someone possibly describe the reason for their dispute in 1-2 sentences?

Per the FCRA, <u>all relevant information must be transmitted to the data furnisher and/or creditor</u>. The credit agencies' online dispute portals ignore this legal requirement and it disrupts the entire federally mandated process!

You have unlimited space to craft your letter, attach supporting documents (which often don't get read) and force them to transmit everything to the data furnisher and/or creditor when you choose to mail or fax your dispute letters to the credit agencies... all while creating a paper trail and not limiting yourself to a computer generated reason for dispute.

The FCRA Expeditious Dispute Resolution

Section 611a(8) of the FCRA revised all consumers' standard protections and requirements of the FCRA when consumers choose to utilize the credit agencies' online dispute process, as follows:

> *"The agency shall not be required to comply with paragraphs 2, 6 and 7 with respect to that dispute if they delete the tradeline within 3 days."*

Paragraph 2

Paragraph 2 requires the credit agencies to forward your dispute AND all its related documentation to the creditor and/or data furnisher. But, the online dispute portals don't allow for any additional paperwork or documentation to be provided... nor considered.

Super Important Info... Right Here!

What you might not be aware of… is that when a credit agency deletes an item without forwarding your dispute to the creditor and/or data furnisher, the creditor and/or data furnisher will report the disputed information again in the next reporting cycle… because the data furnisher and/or creditor wasn't even aware of your dispute!

Plus the creditor and/or data furnisher won't be held liable for failing to send you a notice of its intent to reinsert the disputed item (although a 10-day advance notice of intent to reinsert is required within the FCRA) when the disputed information is reported again.

Paragraph 6

The FCRA requires the credit agencies to provide you with written results… except when you utilize their online dispute portals. Wow… more stripped rights!

Paragraph 7

At your written request, the FCRA requires the credit bureaus to provide you with its method of how it verified the reported information. However, you waive this right when you utilize the credit bureaus' online dispute systems.

And "method of verification" is an extremely powerful tool to utilize… because it can help you hold creditors, data furnishers and credit agencies liable for their actions.

100% Profit Center

And because your online disputes are 100% automated and without any human interaction (including the cheap, outsourced laborers)… they have 100% online dispute profits. How? They still charge data furnishers and/or creditors $0.25 per dispute... for a 100% profit! Hahahahahaaaa!!

Automated Consumer Dispute Verification (ACDV)

When consumers dispute credit report entries online, the credit agencies dispute system generates its 3-digit dispute code, creates a couple lines of narrative and then compiles that data onto a universally recognized template... known as the Automated Consumer Dispute Verification form.

The credit agencies' e-OSCAR system (Online Solution for Complete and Accurate Reporting) has 26 available dispute codes... of which only 5 of the codes are typically used. These codes cannot convey a complete picture of all consumer disputes, and are inadequate because of this limitation.

The automated investigation is initiated by the credit agency sending the ACDV through the e-OSCAR system. A regardless of whether supporting documentation or a detailed description of the dispute was attached, your dispute is reduced to a 3-digit code that's transmitted to the credit agency, data furnisher and/or creditor.

Most Utilized e-OSCAR Codes
- 30.5% not his/hers
- 21.2% disputes account status/history
- 16.8% claims inaccurate information - no specific dispute
- 8.8% disputes amounts
- 7.0% claims account was closed by consumer

Categorizing Disputes

The credit agencies' employees are handcuffed by the limitations of the systems that they have to work within… and more or less have been reduced to simply categorizing disputes as they see fit, without true consideration of your documentation or written statements.

During an FTC hearing, a credit agency employee indicated that when he could choose a category that he felt was sufficient for the complaint… he saw no reason to review the consumers' written text at all.

Agency Depositions

In a March 2007 deposition, Equifax's Vice President of Global Consumer Services described Equifax's re-investigation process, as follows:

Question: What knowledge do you have as to the mechanics of how a DDC (outsourced) Filipino employee would process an Equifax dispute?

Answer: The electronic image would be displayed on their screen. They would have an ACIS (Automated Consumer Interview System) screen that they would use. They would then look at the electronic image. They would read off the identifying information, enter that ID information into the system, and access that credit report. At that point, they'd be able to determine if they were looking at the correct file. If they were, they'd go further. They'd read the letter, they gain an understanding of the issues at hand, and they'd look at the credit report to see if the credit report at that time reflects that. If it does, they would send those particular items to the data furnisher or furnishers. They would request that an investigation be started.

Question: Right. But they're not going to handle whatever response the creditor may provide?

Answer: That's correct.

Question: Do DDC employees have telephones on their desks?

Answer: I do not believe so.

Question: As part of their compliance with Equifax's procedures, do DDC's employees telephone consumers as part of conducting a re-investigation?

Answer: They do not.

Question: Do they telephone creditors, the furnishers, as part of conducting the re-investigation?

Answer: They do not.

Question: Do they telephone anybody from outside DDC or Equifax as part of conducting a re-investigation of a consumer dispute?

Answer: They do not.

Question: What about emailing any of those non-Equifax, non-DDC people, creditors, consumers or third parties?

Answer: They should not be - they do not email them.

Question: And what about fax machines?

Answer: They do not use fax machines.

Question: Under what circumstances will a DDC employee forward the consumer's actual dispute letter or documents they provided to the furnisher or creditor as part of the re-investigation?

Answer: A mechanism does not exist to forward the actual documents.

…and that is exactly why you never want to dispute online!

Challenge, Dispute or Sweep?

It's fundamentally critical that you understand the difference between different credit complaint types and methods. There are primarily three (3) different methods and three (3) different federal laws that are often utilized and/or cited when filing credit verification or information authentication requests with credit agencies, as follows:

The Fair Credit Reporting Act (FCRA), the Fair and Accurate Credit Transactions Act (FACTA) and the Fair Debt Collection Practices Act (FDCPA) as well as some lesser known legal rulings all provide you with some fundamental rights that can help you during your credit restoration process. So, let's explore these a little more deeply.

Fair Credit Reporting Act (FCRA)

The Fair Credit Reporting Act (FCRA) went into effect in 1971, and it outlines your rights as well as outlining all the specific ways that credit agencies must handle your information. Your primary rights given within the framework of this law... are your rights to only have 100% accurate, complete and verifiable information contained within your credit files.

Fair and Accurate Credit Transactions Act (FACTA)

The Fair and Accurate Credit Transactions Act (FACTA) went into effect in 2003. It was meant to help prevent identity theft, simplify the resolution of consumer disputes, improve the accuracy of consumer records, make improvements in the use of (and consumer access to) credit information, as well as for other purposes.

Fair Debt Collection Practices Act (FDCPA)

The Fair Debt Collection Practices Act (FDCPA) is a federal law that Congress enacted to protect people from abusive, deceptive or unfair debt collection practices.

The FDCPA forces collection companies, creditors, etc. to validate debts owed within very specific guidelines… and has resulted in numerous, major monetary judgments & settlements from collection agencies and creditors that have violated the FDCPA.

Challenges

A credit challenge is more of a "yes, it's mine" but I'm complaining because I feel the information being reported is less than 100% accurate, complete and verifiable. This method is theoretically safer, because you aren't perjuring yourself by stating that it wasn't yours to begin with.

However, everyone in the credit repair business will tell you that it seems as if the credit agencies really don't even read your letters… and there's some truth to it too!

In an earlier chapter, I mentioned the ACDV for that automates and activates the e-OSCAR system. And e-OSCAR utilizes OCR to determine what the "true purpose" of your letter is… and then assigns a 3-digit code and then transmits it to the creditors and awaits the creditors' responses.

But I will say, that I ethically feel that challenge letters are far more ethical... than making a broad, blanket statement for a consumer that might intentionally or inadvertently state they've never had an account with a specific creditor.

Disputes

A dispute letter isn't necessarily always a claim of never having had an account, living at an address or not applying for credit with a specific creditor.

A dispute letter can also state that you're demanding a reinvestigation of information on the basis of something not being 100% accurate, complete and verifiable.

But there have been instances where a consumer has been subpoenaed for a court hearing due to their dispute of information on their credit report. So, whatever you do... never blatantly lie about what occurred in the past. Simply stay within the scope of the law. And remember that your debt is your debt... regardless of how old the debt is.

Credit Sweeps

A credit sweep is far worse than a dispute! And in my opinion (as well as the FTC's) it's downright immoral, unethical and illegal.

Have you ever seen a credit repair company advertise their guarantee that they can remove or delete 100% of your bad credit (usually within 30-90 days)?!! You should report them to the FTC, Bureau of Consumer Financial Protection and your state Attorney General immediately if you ever see claims like these... because 1) it's illegal to guarantee specific results (regardless of their success rate) and 2) they're more than likely utilizing fake police reports (or police reports that they coach you to obtain) to falsely claim that each of your negative items were due to you being the victim of Identity Theft.

However, if you were truly the victim of Identity Theft... it is 100% legal to utilize legitimate police reports to dispute specific negative accounts, where you never applied for credit.

Credit sweeps are wrong and do more harm than good. The risk of producing fake documentation or lying to credit agencies just isn't worth it, because credit sweeps can cost you thousands more in legal fees plus jail time... when or if your past creditors subpoena you for a court hearing and you're convicted of perjury.

Pay... or Do It Yourself?

Before we get into whether it's better to pay for someone else to help you repair, restore, fix or rebuild your credit ratings... you have rights!

If you're paying someone else to repair your credit, they are automatically considered a credit repair organization (unless the person operates as an attorney or 501(c)3 non-profit organization) and must be licensed and possibly bonded... depending upon your state.

All credit repair organizations must provide the following disclosure notice to you, as well as retain copies of your records and signed disclosures for a period of at least two (2) years.

Consumer File Rights Under State and Federal Law

You have a right to dispute inaccurate information in your credit report by contacting the credit bureau directly. However, neither you nor any "credit repair" company or credit repair organization has the right to have accurate, current, and verifiable information removed from your credit report. The credit bureau must remove accurate, negative information from your report only if it is over 7 years old. Bankruptcy information can be reported for 10 years.

You have a right to obtain a copy of your credit report from a credit bureau. You may be charged a reasonable fee. There is no fee, however, if you have been turned down for credit, employment, insurance, or a rental dwelling because of information in your credit report within the preceding 60 days. The credit bureau must provide someone to help you interpret the information in your credit file. You are entitled to receive a free copy of your credit report if you are unemployed and intend to apply for employment in the next 60 days, if you are a recipient of public welfare assistance, or if you have reason to believe that there is inaccurate information in your credit report due to fraud.

You have a right to sue a credit repair organization that violates the Credit Repair Organization Act. This law prohibits deceptive practices by credit repair organizations.

You have the right to cancel your contract with any credit repair organization for any reason within 3 business days from the date you signed it.

Credit bureaus are required to follow reasonable procedures to ensure that the information they report is accurate. However, mistakes may occur.

You may, on your own, notify a credit bureau in writing that you dispute the accuracy of information in your credit file. The credit bureau must then reinvestigate and modify or remove inaccurate or incomplete information. The credit bureau may not charge any fee for this service. Any pertinent information and copies of all documents you have concerning an error should be given to the credit bureau.

If the credit bureau's reinvestigation does not resolve the dispute to your satisfaction, you may send a brief statement to the credit bureau, to be kept in your file, explaining why you think the record is inaccurate. The credit bureau must include a summary of your statement about disputed information with any report it issues about you.

The Federal Trade Commission regulates credit bureaus and credit repair organizations. For more information contact:

The Public Reference Branch
 Federal Trade Commission
 Washington, D.C. 20580

Paid Services to Credit Repair Organizations

There are numerous, highly reputable credit repair organizations that are operated by credit professionals throughout the US. The best ones are often participating members of The National Association of Credit Service Organizations (NACSO). These types of credit professionals tend to truly care, are extremely knowledgeable, continue to invest in their knowledge of credit regulations, keep up with the latest industry news, they'll usually refrain from doing anything that violates credit repair regulations and they often get great results for their clients and referral partners.

However... there can be bad apples that damage entire industry reputations... such companies that advertise "we guaranteed credit removal" or charge illegal upfront fees. And sometimes newer, smaller companies simply try to service too many clients, begin to fall behind, and can't answer every customer's phone call.

Additionally, I've never liked companies that charge monthly subscription fees for their credit services... which some of the biggest credit repair companies do! The problem I have with this practice, is twofold.

Monthly subscription fee services will often only help you challenge or dispute 2-3 items per month... designed to drag your services out as long as possible. This primarily benefits the credit repair organization. And the FTC and some Attorney Generals have a problem with this type of business practice (or business model), because many months can go by where a consumer has not successfully had any credit improvements or negative items removed from their credit files… which constitutes being paid an advance fee prior to rendering successful credit repair services.

In my opinion, the most reputable credit repair organizations only require payment for the successful deletion of each negative item , from each of your credit reports. And to combat the issue of non-payment from some customers, some credit service organizations will require an upfront payment that's held in a separate trust account (that's administered by a 3rd party) and is billed for payments as services are successfully rendered per a written and signed contract.

Do It Yourself Credit Repair

While you definitely have the right to challenge or dispute credit information yourself, consider that many attorneys seek out the assistance of seasoned credit repair veterans on a daily basis… as it's too much hassle!

While a botched brain surgery and failed credit repair can certainly have two entirely different outcomes… the consequences are both extremely painful in their own ways.

Which leads to… **why would you try to repair your own credit**, when you might not truly understand everything there is to know about credit reports, scores, laws and how to deal with the creditors', collection agencies' and credit agencies' notorious stall tactics?!

But what about the expense of paying someone else for credit repair?!! I've outlines some typical fees or expenses you might have to pay… if you utilize a credit repair company.

- $0 - $100 Account Setup Fee
- $19 - $49 Monthly Credit Monitoring Fee
- $150 - $300 Credit Audit / Analysis Fee
- $79 - $149 Monthly Subscription
- $50 - $100 Per Deletion (often averaging between $1000 to $3000 or more)

So if you utilized a "monthly subscription" credit repair service for 6-12 months, you'll typically pay somewhere between $738 to $2,776. Or if you utilized a "per deletion" credit repair service for 6-12 months, you'll typically pay somewhere between $1,264 to $3,988 (or more). And some companies have a maximum fee structure that limits your total financial outlay for the monthly subscription fees and/or the deleted items.

Obviously your total expenses have alot to do with your decision to try to repair your own credit... or to utilize trusted experts.

And I'd still always recommend placing your credit repair in the trusted hands of a highly, reputable credit expert... as the future saving of lower interest rates, lower payments and reduced embarrassment (or job loss) will far outweigh the costs associated.

But... Is There An Even Better Way?

You might want to download the CreditUturn mobile app... which eliminates the majority of your credit repair expenses (except your credit monitoring fee), automatically analyzes your credit reports, makes credit challenge recommendations, automatically prepares your challenge (or dispute) letters, allows you edit or recreate your letters, submits your approved letters for you, continues to monitor your credit reports each month, compares your credit reports (looking for any changes) and starts the cycle all over again!

Plus, it also gives you credit rebuilding recommendations... and let's you know when you might be ready to purchase your new car or home!

And all for a small $39 monthly credit monitoring fee... that you can cancel at any time, without any long term contracts. It's secure & very easy to use!

Go to https://CreditUturn.com and register for your free download to get started, today!

And when you utilize the CreditUturn mobile app yourself & recommend it to your friends... you're helping make a positive change within the credit repair industry!

Like I said before, there are a handful of reputable credit repair companies sprinkled across the United States. But in the wonderful day & age of automation that we live in... why pay exorbitant fees to someone else for services that are automated and you can control?

Catch Them In A Lie

When challenging credit information, it's very important to formulate a plan of exactly how you're going to attack the inaccurate, incomplete or unverifiable information.

Should you dispute online? This usually isn't the recommended option.

Should you write a complaint to your state Attorney General, the Bureau of Consumer Financial Protection (formerly known as the CFPB) or the Federal Trade Commission (FTC)? It doesn't hurt, but these agencies will force you to utilize online dispute systems... if you file the complaint online.

Should you write a letter directly to (or call) the creditor? Maybe... if you've been a great customer of the creditor for years and are simply asking them to remove a reported late payment. Anything bigger than that... most credit professionals will recommend that you dispute it directly with the credit agencies.

Should you write a letter directly to (or call) the collection agency? Some credit repair companies advocate sending "Debt Validation" letters to collection agencies... hoping that the collection agency can't locate your records, produces lesser balances, different (inaccurate) account information, etc. However, be prepared for updated collection activity to increase (including up to a court summons) and/or the dreaded, updated Date of Last Activity (DLA) to be reported to the credit bureaus for the account… which might lower your credit score, due to what appears to be a newly reported collection account.

By the way… debt validation letters can be a great tactic to use. Just know the risk! It helps when the reported collection account is past your state's Statute of Limitations. And know that your debt is always your debt, even if the Statute of Limitations has expired… because the Statute of Limitations only governs whether the creditor can seek judgment against you for future wage garnishment, assignments, etc.

Should you write a letter directly to (or call) the credit agencies? This is the most common tactic, and most universally accept method of credit challenges or disputes. And these types of challenges or disputes usually don't trigger updated Dates of Last Activity (DLA) when your letters are regarding collection accounts… unless you request a debt validation.

And if you receive a court summons to appear regarding a disputed debt (that was only disputed with the credit agencies)… it was probably in the process of happening already.

Should I freeze my credit reports? Yes and no.

Yes, you should freeze the 3 major credit agencies… if you've been the victim of or are truly concerned about Identity Theft.

But no… you should not freeze the 3 major credit agencies.. if you think it'll help you repair your credit.

However, because this chapter is titled '**Catch Them In A Lie**', it can help you to freeze smaller credit agencies' (also known as sub-agencies) files. Why? Remember that the smaller agencies collect data and resell

CATCH THEM IN A LIE

that data to the 3 major credit reporting agencies. And when the smaller secondary agencies' have frozen your credit files... they no longer have permission to share, sell or verify your credit information.

When responding to your previous credit challenges, the 3 major credit agencies will often respond with "Account Verified", "Account Confirmed", "Verified", etc. And even though your previous letter may have asked for proof of its utilized verification methods, the credit agencies will often violate the FCRA by not including it.

So then you should send them a new letter stating that you didn't proof of how it verified your disputed account information, and request copies of all the information too. They will often reply that they verified the information with the sub-agency that furnished the data. Hmmmm..... wait, what??! They can't do that. And therein lies the trap that was set.

Now, some people might disagree with the tactic... but it's part of the way the law's written. And if you disagree, would you prefer to continue to have misreported, inaccurate, incomplete or unverifiable information reported... or play the game by their rules? Exactly!

And don't forget... the credit agencies and/or creditors will often send insufficient account validations back to you as well. Simply mailing back the last billing statement is unsufficient... when ALL contracts, payment records and other correspondence are required to meet the true definition of debt validation.

Eliminate Your Money & Credit Fears

Having 700+ (or even 800+) credit scores is a very empowering feeling! And assuming you have sufficient income, little debt and your loan amount is reasonable… knowing that you'll never feel the embarrassment of hearing "Sorry, you've been denied." is awesome!

And who wouldn't want to be able to help their children or grandchildren, be able to start a business, travel when desired, rent a car or get a hotel room when a hurricane hits?

You see… credit is an absolute necessity, regardless of what Dave Ramsey says! And while I certainly agree that you should be fiscally responsible and carry as little debt as possible… the credit game forces you to enter into and repay debt on an occasional basis.

Why is credit so important?

Try to pay cash for a rental car without a credit card, unless you're perfectly okay with allowing them to put a hold on your bank account (for anywhere from $500 and up to your entire account balance). And the same can hold true for flights, hotels, etc.

Furthermore, credit cards give you some added protection… in the form of life insurance, cancellations, refunds, etc. that cash and/or debit cards don't provide.

Additionally, having no credit is just like having bad credit... especially when getting quoted for auto insurance, because you're a greater risk to the insurance companies if they're unable to view an excellent credit file score.

And how about the people that have been victims of natural disasters like wildfires... that need to buy a new car, house, clothes, etc? Sure, there insurance company will help them somewhat... but how long will it take for claims to be paid, will the settlements be enough, etc?

While having cash on hand is nice... it also isn't always the smartest financial move. And when your cash is tied up in the stock market, it can take you days or weeks to sell your stock... and then you're often waiting for the bank to release funds from the huge check you received in the mail.

And with great credit, you can be approved for manufacturer specials on new cars that offer zero (0%) financing. But without a credit score... you might not even obtain a loan!

So the bottom line is... be thrifty, frugal, financially savvy, aware and be credit wise!

Is Business Credit Important?

When you're first starting your business, it's easy to pay for things you need from your personal checking account or credit cards. But as your business grows, you'll find that there are numerous benefits to having business credit… and it's in your best interest to create separate financial accounts for your business.

Separating Your Personal and Business Accounts

When you have a separate business account, it's easier to track your business expenses. You'll be less likely to pierce your corporate veil… because you didn't have a purchase that combined your business and personal expenses. And although your business' credit approvals might initially be based on your personal credit score… your business will eventually build its own Dun & Bradstreet (DNB) Paydex score. This means that your own credit rating isn't directly tied to the success, or failure, of your business.

Additionally, utilizing business credit may give your business some additional tax advantages as well as reducing (if not eliminating) your personal liability against lawsuits and possibly even protecting your personal assets.

Business Loans

Improving your business credit score means that banks will be more likely to give you the money you need to purchase new equipment or expand your business. Banks will be able to easily check your financial statements, both income and expenses, to determine how much your business can afford. And your approved business loan amounts are often 5-10 times larger, than if you were trying to get a loan as an individual.

Rewards

Many business credit cards offer rewards, such as cash back on all purchases or airline miles that you can use for free flights. In effect, this saves your business money on everything that you need to run your business.

Extended Warranty Protection

Some banks will offer an additional extended warranty term (at no additional charge) on items that you purchase with your business credit card, as well as other protections. This lets you buy essential equipment without worrying whether it will break on you.

Tracking Expenses

If you only make purchases using your business accounts—checks, credit or debit cards—you'll be able to easily track those expenses. In fact, you won't have to save your receipts for tax time. You can simply use the copy of your business' checking and/or credit card statements for the year.

Financing Capabilities

If you have a business credit card or line of credit, you can finance a purchase that you need to make for your business, usually at a fairly low interest rate. In fact, many business credit cards offer a zero percent interest rate for a certain time period.

Let's Get Started... with 8 Simple Steps

1) Incorporate

Even though you may be incorporated when you're reading this, it deserves a mention. Incorporating a business or forming an LLC creates a business that is legally separate from the owner(s).

Sole proprietors and general partnerships are legally the same as being a person. So these don't provide a separation of business credit history from personal.

2) Employer Identification Number (EIN)

The EIN is basically a social security number for a business. It is required on federal tax filings, and is also required to open a business bank account in the name of the corporation or LLC. In order to comply with IRS requirements, many larger businesses also require an EIN from their vendors in order to pay them for services provided.

3) Open a Business Bank Account

Open a business checking account in the legal business name. Once open, be sure to pay the financial transactions of the business from that account. And always be sure to pay the credit card bill... only from your business checking account. Do not mix!

4) Establish a Business Phone Number

Whether you use landline, cell phone or VoIP services, you must have a separate number only in your business's legal name. List that number in the directory so it can be found.

5) Open a Business Credit File

Contact Dun & Bradstreet (DNB), Experian, Equifax and TransUnion to create business credit files in your company's legal name.

6) Get a Vendor Line of Credit

Apply with five (5) vendors and/or suppliers to create credit lines for your company to use, when purchasing with them. Ask them to report your payment history to the credit reporting agencies. And some major office supply stores are also great places to establish credit with, and remember to only utilize your company's EIN number when applying... unless you want to also be personally liable as a guarantor.

7) Apply for a Business Credit Card

Obtain at least one business credit card that is not linked to you or any other owners personally. Companies like CitiBank, American Express, Discover, etc. typically provide excellent business credit cards.

8) Pay Your Bills on Time

Perhaps it should go unsaid, but be sure to pay your bills on time. Like with your personal credit, late payments will negatively impact your business credit. And unlike personal credit information that only shows a late payment on your credit report after it's been late for 30+ days... business credit reports will show payment histories as late after only 1 day!

Wealth Accumulation Mode

From this day forward (if you haven't already been doing this), promise yourself… to always be in "rack & stack mode"!

Pay your bills, limit your expenses, open a completely different bank account (even at a completely separate bank) that you deposit ALL your extra cash into and **that you never touch**… except to use for smart investments or for *EXTREME* emergencies.

You're Not a Financial Wreck

You and millions of people never were truly educated about money, how to save, planning, budgeting or the real power of compound interest. But, we're all taught to be consumers… of the latest fads, clothing, cars, electronics, movies, travel, entertainment and restaurants.

Struggling to Pay Your Bills

Be honest with yourself. Sit down, write out all your expenses. Monitor exactly what you're truly spending. Millions of people waste hundreds if not thousands each month… on lottery tickets, Starbucks, fast food, fine dining, movies, alcohol, drugs, clothing addictions, etc.

Now, I'm not saying you have a problem… because I certainly don't know you. So assess yourself. And I mean really put yourself under a microscope… or get a friend or family member to help you. The pain will be short term.

And once you realize the areas you can start to reduce expenses, you'll also need to assess what steps you can take to increase your income. Do you have a hidden talent? Could you be promoted with a renewed zest in your career? Should you finish your degree? What about that business you always wanted to start? The possibilities are endless.

And I highly recommend the book 'You Need More Money' (subtitled: Wake Up and Solve Your Financial Problems Once and For All) by Matt Monero. It's full of real talk, wisdom and insight from a multi-millionaire… that struggled until he had his "Aha!" moment.

Swallow Some Humble Pie

Every now and then, we have to swallow our pride (humble pie) and do things that we might feel are beneath us. I know multi-millionaires that used to (and some still do) buy and sell items from yard sales, flea markets and bargain stores… to resell on eBay and Craigslist. Why? Because they had dreams and also knew they had to kickstart their inner "rack & stack" mode!

The ways you can increase your income are virtually limitless… and are only limited by your thinking or willingness to do what it takes to OVERCOME!

Close Your Eyes

Just imagine that you eliminated only $500 of unnecessary monthly expenses, plus you were also earning another $1,000 to $2,000 per month or more.

Stay with me! Now visualize (and I mean see yourself walking through

71

the front doors, across the lobby floor, smiling at the bank teller and depositing ANOTHER regular deposit into your special "no touch" investment account. Now… that's what I call "rack & stack"!

It's an amazing feeling to know that you're turning things around, and it's my hope that in some small way… I'm able to be the catalyst that ignites your inner flame to fix your finances and your credit too!

CreditUturn Members Group

Of course you do! Who doesn't? Now, I'm not saying you're incapable of doing this on your own. But it certainly helps to have a cheerleader in your corner… or to be your voice of reason. Use the CreditUturn Facebook Private Members Group, where you'll find thousands of supporters, cheerleaders and some real talk to help you rise from the ashes!

More Money = Better Credit

Having more money equals better credit, because now you'll have the mindset to always find a way to get your bills paid on time. Have you ever heard someone say the banks won't loan you money… until you don't need it. Well, there's alot of truth to that.

You see… alot of people with better credit (your unknown millionaires that have nice 401k retirement plans, own some of their employer's stock, etc.) will only utilize credit to get better terms that cost less than what they can earn by investing the same dollars elsewhere.

Now, you might not be able to adopt that strategy from Day 1 of your credit rebuild. But you can get there faster than you think by eating some humble pie, plugging the leaks in your expenses, investing in your education, getting the promotion you want… and by stashing money into your completely separate bank account that's constantly growing.

Recommended Books

You Need More Money - by Matt Manero

Build A Rental Property Empire - by Mark Ferguson

The Greatest Salesman in the World - by Og Mandino

Think and Grow Rich - by Napolean Hill

Rich Dad Poor Dad - by Robert Kiyosaki

How to Win Friends and Influence People - by Dale Carnegie

The Richest Man in Babylon - by George Clason

The 10X Rule - by Grant Cardone

The Secret - by Rhonda Byrne

Sell or Be Sold - by Grant Cardone

How to Master the Art of Selling - by Tom Hopkins

Be Obsessed or Be Average - by Grant Cardone

Low Profile Selling: Act Like a Lamb Sell Like a Lion - by Tom Hopkins

The Power of Relentless - by Wayne Allyn Root

eSCAPE: The 4 Stages of Becoming a Successful Entrepreneur - by Anik Singal

DotCom Secrets - by Russell Brunson and Dan Kennedy

Expert Secrets - by Russell Brunson and Robert Kiyosaki

How You Can Make a Difference

First of all, thanks for downloading and reading my book 'The Credit Score Game'. And by now… hopefully you've figured out that it's not all completely your fault either!

I wrote this book, developed the CreditUturn mobile app and started a Facebook community that's on a mission and is dedicated toward improving the credit industry, creating more credit awareness (from an early age) and empowering you to rise above whatever of life's challenges may have knocked you down.

Let's Make a Difference!

There are thousands of different credit scoring formulas, and it just confuses everyone. And it will continue to cause more financial meltdowns, as long as Wall Street, institutional investors, pension funds and everyday citizens don't truly know that momentary credit score is truly reflecting… especially when thousands of mortgages are lumped together and sold as mortgage pools.

In order to combat this, I truly believe there should be 1 universally adopted credit score formula (nationwide, not regionally), per industry type (1 formula specifically for autos, 1 for mortgages, 1 for personal loans, and 1 for credit cards) per credit agency… so that every lender can easily be able to determine how to price their loan approvals accordingly.

This would make it easier for Wall Street to truly grade the risk associated with buying mortgage pools & technically safer for institutional investors to make better decisions.

And government watchdogs, such as: our elected officials, the Federal Trade Commission (FTC), the Bureau for Consumer Financial Protection, and the U.S. Attorney General should require this simplicity... for the sake of better consumer disclosure and awareness.

Penalties for Paying Off Collections

And why are the credit agencies penalizing everyone that pays off old collection accounts? It doesn't make any sense... and needs to change!

You should be rewarded for doing the right thing, when you payoff old collections... especially when you realize that paying off an old collection is an indicator that you are NOT getting ready to file for bankruptcy protection. Right?!!

So your credit score should increase as collection balances are reduced & even more once they're paid off... and possibly deleted as soon as they're paid in full too. The system is broken when consumers are penalized for paying a collection to a $0 balance... simply because the "reporting clock" is updated to a more recent date of "collection" activity.

Think About It

Congress created a federal law in 1968, The Truth in Lending Act (**TILA**), to protect consumers in their dealings with lenders and creditors. So why not also protect everyone (plus investors) in their dealings with FICO, VantageScore and the credit agencies too?

The fact is that the credit agencies actually might wield more power than Big Pharma, and it's still much more lucrative to continue peddling custom scoring models to banks. More credit scoring confusion… creates more credit requests. And more credit requests = BILLIONS in annual revenue!

Recommend CreditUturn to Everyone You Know

I am 100% committed to helping your voice be heard in Washington, DC and within every legislator's office throughout the United States… to raise awareness, improve our credit systems, continue fighting discriminatory practices and simplify disclosures that make it easier for everyone to understand.

We'll be working alongside credit industry partners to fight for positive changes within the credit and financial world. And it'll be easier to do with your full support!

Thanks again for downloading or ordering my book, and I sincerely hope to be a part of making a positive difference in your life!

About the Author

Lee Kendrick is a 30-year veteran of the automotive and mortgage industries, has viewed 500,000+ credit reports, and also has an additional 25+ years of credit repair experience. Having grown up in a middle-class family, living paycheck-to-paycheck and witnessing the closure of major manufacturing facilities and its effect on small communities… he decided to learn everything he could about credit laws & your rights! And rather than help a few hundred people with their free CreditUturn™ each month, Lee has recently founded & launched the CreditUturn mobile app that analyzes your credit reports, makes recommendations, prepares credit dispute letters, submits your letters to creditors and/or credit agencies, tracks your progress, and continues cycling through your reports each month… without any credit repair fees. You simply need to download the app, sign up for its recommended credit monitoring service and take control of your credit!

You can connect with me on:

- https://CreditUturn.com
- https://twitter.com/CreditUturn
- https://facebook.com/CreditUturn
- https://instagram.com/CreditUturn
- https://youtube.com/CreditUturn
- https://linkedin.com/in/CreditUturn

Also by Lee Kendrick

The Credit Score Game: It's Not Your Fault

Credit scores are a necessity of life, but thousands of credit scoring formulas exist. Yes, you have to pay your bills on time and establish a good mix of credit types to obtain excellent credit scores. But your credit scores are controlled and manipulated by credit agencies, such as: how lengthy of a credit history do you have, did your banks reports your good credit to all the major credit agencies, did the credit agencies mix someone else's credit information into your files, did an auto dealership or mortgage company blast your credit application to 22 banks, etc? Plus when you factor in that most lenders loan approval standards vary drastically from one institution to the next... it's really NOT your fault!

www.ingramcontent.com/pod-product-compliance
Lightning Source LLC
Chambersburg PA
CBHW071115210326
41519CB00020B/6304